Bonjour, Piano!

ISBN 978-1-4950-8868-1

DURAND SALABERT ESCHIG
Editions Musicales

Visit Hal Leonard Online at
www.halleonard.com

CONTENTS

iv **COMPOSER BIOGRAPHIES**
viii **POINTS FOR PRACTICE AND TEACHING**

OLIVIER HAURAY
6   Franz
16 Mystery

CHARLES KOECHLIN
from *Ten Easy Little Pieces*
5   Greetings
17 Lullaby
27 Siciliana

DARIUS MILHAUD
22 Candy from *A Child Loves*

FRANCIS POULENC
from *The Villagers*
12 Staccato
10 Tyrolean Waltz

MAURICE RAVEL
28 Prélude

PIERRE SANCAN
from *For Small Hands*
18 Skipping
20 Sound the Drum

ERIK SATIE
7   Gymnopédie No. 1 from *Three Gymnopédies*

HENRI SAUGUET
14 Paul and Virginia from *Poetic Pieces,* Book 2

DÉODAT DE SÉVERAC
24 Games in the Park from *On Vacation,* Volume 1

ALEXANDRE TANSMAN
from *For Children*, Volume 2
31 The Little Cartoon Cat
from *For Children*, Volume 3
32 Difficult Problem
2   Ping Pong
from *Ten Diversions for the Young Pianist*
26 Dreams
4   Prayer
30 Spanish Mood

Editorial suggestions in the music appear in brackets.

COMPOSER BIOGRAPHIES

OLIVIER HAURAY
(b. 1952)

Olivier Hauray was trained in organ and piano at the Caen Conservatory and with private teachers, and studied musicology at the Sorbonne. His career has been dedicated entirely to teaching piano; *Introduction to the piano by styles* volumes 1 and 2 are the result of his experiences as pedagogue confronted with the difficulties that student pianists have to solve. The books contain Hauray's original pedagogical pieces, emulating musical styles from Baroque to jazz, and proposing the technical solutions for their expressive purpose. Olivier Hauray continues to compose according to his musical encounters and his educational projects.

CHARLES KOECHLIN
(1867-1950)

Charles Koechlin was a prolific composer of diverse inspiration, ranging from impressionistic style to more chromatic, even quasi-serial techniques. He was born in Paris and attended the Paris Conservatoire, studying composition with Jules Massenet and later with Gabriel Fauré. His relationship with Fauré extended to writing the first Fauré biography and orchestrating Faure's suite from *Pelléas et Mélisande*. During his time as a freelance composer and teacher, Koechlin participated in several musical societies including the *Société musicale independent* and the International Society for Contemporary Music (ISCM). Koechlin made several trips to the United States with a special focus on the University of California, Berkeley. On his third trip in 1929, his symphonic poem *La Joie païenne* won the Hollywood Bowl Prize for Composition. Though rejected for a teaching position at the Conservatoire, he did join the faculty at the Schola Cantorum from 1935-1939.

DARIUS MILHAUD
(1892-1974)

Darius Milhaud was a noted member of Les Six, a group of composers whose music was perceived as a reaction to both French Impressionism and extended Romanticism. His extremely large output of music (his opus list ended at 443) bears influences from both American jazz and Brazilian dance music. Like many other composers featured in this publication, he studied at the Paris Conservatoire. From 1917 to 1919, he worked as secretary to Paul Claudel, a poet and playright who also happened to be the French ambassador to Brazil. Milhaud and Claudel collaborated on many artistic projects, and the contact also allowed him the opportunity to travel to Brazil and become inspired by the popular music he heard there. Two significant works resulted from this experience: *Le boeuf sur le toit* (1920), a ballet full of Brazilian tunes, and *Saudades do Brasil* (1920), a piano suite of dances inspired by neighborhoods in Rio de Janeiro. Likewise, a 1922 trip to the United States, where Milhaud heard jazz in Harlem, provided the inspiration for the ballet suite *La creation du monde* (1923). Milhaud married his cousin Madeleine and they had a child. The Nazi invasion of France prompted them to flee to the United States in 1940. He began teaching at Mills College in Oakland, where his students included jazz pianist Dave Brubeck. After the war he was able to return to Paris and resume teaching at the Conservatoire until his retirement.

FRANCIS POULENC
(1899-1963)

A member of Les Six, Poulenc was born into a wealthy family of pharmaceutical manufacturers in Paris. He attended the Lycée Condorcet, a secondary school, instead of entering a conservatory. In Poulenc's early explorations of music, Debussy, Schubert, and Stravinsky made especially large impressions. His mother, an amateur pianist, gave him lessons from age 5 to 16, when he began formal studies with Ricardo Viñes. Poulenc's mother died that year, and his father died two years later. Viñes now became more of a mentor, and encouraged Poulenc to compose. He also helped Poulenc to meet the composers Auric and Satie. After serving in the French army from 1918 to 1921, Poulenc began composition lessons with Charles Koechlin. He also became an accompanist to baritone Pierre Bernac, who would later premiere many of Poulenc's art songs. A devout Catholic, Poulenc composed several sacred choral works, including a Mass in G, *Stabat Mater*, and *Gloria*. He also composed operas, ballets, film scores, orchestral pieces, chamber music, art songs, and piano music. In 1936 his composer friend Pierre-Octave Ferroud was killed in a particularly violent car accident, and this caused Poulenc to take a pilgrimage to the commune of Rocamadour, which contains some of the oldest churches in France. Following this journey, he brought a new seriousness and depth of religious feeling to his compositions. The most notable feature of Poulenc's music is his true gift for melody. Even his non-vocal works abound with fresh tunes, and these are paired with sensitive harmonic turns that carry his unique stamp.

MAURICE RAVEL
(1875–1937)

Ravel is, along with Debussy, considered the most important French composer of the twentieth century. He was raised in Paris but born in Ciboure, a Basque villa in the southwestern corner of France to Swiss and Basque parents. His lifelong use of exotic influences in his music stemmed from his heritage-based affinity for Basque and Spanish culture. Ravel studied piano and then composition with Gabriel Fauré at the Paris Conservatoire, though he was dismissed for not meeting the necessary requirements in either piano or composition. This, along with his heritage, may have influenced the lack of support he received from French music critics and the Société Nationale de Musique, Paris' leading concert society. Critics often pitted him unfavorably against Debussy and accused him of copying Debussy's style. In 1909, Ravel founded the Société Musicale Indépendente in opposition to the Société Nationale, naming Fauré president. This society strove to organize performances of both French and foreign works regardless of their style or genre. The same year he wrote *Daphnis et Chloé* for famed choreographer Diaghilev and began his close friendship with Igor Stravinsky. He joined the army as a driver in the motor transport corps during World War I, a tragic time in which he was also deeply affected by the loss of his mother, with whom he was extremely close. He lived the rest of his life thirty miles west of Paris in Montfort l'Amaury surrounded by the Forest of Rambouillet, travelling around Europe and North America performing and attending premieres of his works. Ravel is remembered as a supreme orchestrator. His orchestration of Mussorgsky's *Pictures at an Exhibition* holds a place in standard orchestral repertoire, as does *Bolero*, his most famous piece and a textbook example of his skills in orchestration.

PIERRE SANCAN
(1916-2008)

After early piano studies in Morocco and Toulouse, Sancan moved to Paris and studied with Yves Nat at the Conservatoire. He won several awards for his skills in composition and counterpoint, including the prestigious Prix de Rome in 1943 for his cantata *La Légende de Icare*. He achieved a teaching post at the Conservatoire in 1956, when Yves Nat retired. As a pianist, Sancan was highly regarded, though most of his public appearances were accompanying the cellist André Navarra. Sancan's compositions include an opera *Ondine* (1962), two ballets, two piano concertos, and advanced pieces for piano.

ERIK SATIE
(1866-1925)

One of the most eccentric personalities in all of music, Satie began piano studies in 1874, with a teacher who instilled a love of medieval music and chant. He entered the Paris Conservatoire in 1878, and was expelled two and a half years later for lack of talent. He was readmitted in 1885, but did not change the minds of his professors. After a detour in the Infantry – seen for a moment as a better career choice – Satie settled in the artistic Paris neighborhood of Montmartre in 1887. There he composed his first pieces: *Ogives*, for piano, written without barlines (a compositional choice found frequently in Satie's music) and the famous *Gymnopédies*. In 1890, while pianist and conductor at the cabaret Le Chat Noir, he met Claude Debussy and joined the spiritual movement Rose-Croix du Sâr Péladan (Rosicrucian Order), eventually becoming a choirmaster for the group. His involvement inspired the works *Sonneries de la Rose+Croix* and *Le Fils des Etoiles.* He had a brief and passionate relationship with the painter Suzanne Valadon in 1893. Brokenhearted after Suzanne left, he wrote *Vexations*, a theme to be played 840 times in a row – about twenty hours. In 1895 Satie abandoned his usual red robe and replaced it with seven identical mustard velvet suits, nicknaming himself "the Velvet Gentleman." In the next few years he moved to the suburb of Arcueil, and began taking composition lessons at the Schola Cantorum. He met Jean Cocteau, with whom he collaborated on the ballet *Parade* in 1916. Satie gradually met more artists of the French avant-garde, and presided over the birth of the group "Les Six." He died in 1925 of cirrhosis of the liver – probably due to his abundant consumption of absinthe. His friends visited his room in Arcueil – to which he had denied access throughout his life – and they discovered the state of poverty in which Satie had always lived.

HENRI SAUGUET
(1901- 1989)

Born Henri-Pierre Poupard, he used his mother's maiden name Sauguet when he began concertizing, to avoid embarrassing his father with activities in modern music. He studied the piano from an early age, and in 1916 became organist and choirmaster at Floirac near Bordeaux, taking organ lessons with Paul Combes. He studied composition first with Joseph Canteloube and later with Charles Koechlin. In his early career he met other notable composers such as Satie and Milhaud. Sauguet was a noted opera composer, with *La chartreuse de Parme* (1939) his largest-scale work in this vein. He composed several others over the course of his career, and for his first, *Le plumet du colonel* (1924), he even wrote the libretto. Sauguet also found success writing ballets, including *Les forains* (1945), about a traveling circus troupe. During the war, Sauguet used his status to help his many Jewish friends, while still producing an impressive amount of music, including his *Symphonie expiatoire* (1945), dedicated to the innocent victims of the war. Aside from composition, Sauguet was active as a critic for the French journals *L'Europe nouvelle, Le jour,* and *La bataille*. In 1976 he was elected to the Académie des Beaux-Arts in succession to Milhaud. He served as President of several organizations, among them the Union des Compositeurs, which he founded.

DÉODAT DE SÉVÉRAC
(1872-1921)

Sévérac was born in the former Languedoc region of France. He studied with Vincent d'Indy and Albéric Magnard at the Schola Cantorum in Paris, and later worked as an assistant to the Spanish composer Isaac Albéniz. He spent the remainder of his life in southern France. His opera *Héliogabale*, which included parts for some of the folk musicians from his beloved rural provinces, was produced at Béziers in 1910. Séverac is noted for writing vocal and choral music that included settings of verse in the Provençal and Catalan languages. He wrote several collections of piano miniatures, including *Chant de la terre, En Languedoc*, and *En vacances*. His thesis at the Schola Cantorum, La centralization et les petites chapelles en musique, concerned the future of French music; he argued strongly for French composers to draw upon regional folk music sources to protect against the impact of foreign musical influences. Shortly before his death, Sévérac planned to start a music school in the region between Marseilles and Barcelona.

ALEXANDRE TANSMAN
(1897-1986)

Tansman was born in Łódź, Poland, but lived in France for most of his life. While in Poland he trained in music at the Łódź Conservatory and completed a doctorate in law at the University of Warsaw (1918). After moving to Paris in 1920, he met Stravinsky and Ravel, both of whom encouraged his work. Tansman found his way into the Ecole de Paris, a group of foreign musicians that included Bohuslav Martinů. Tansman enjoyed international success, with his orchestral music performed under such esteemed conductors as Koussevitzky, Toscanini, and Stokowski. During an American concert tour as pianist with Koussevitzky and the Boston Symphony in 1927, Tansman met George Gershwin. His concertizing also took him to Europe, Asia, Palestine and India, where he was a guest of Mahatma Gandhi in 1933. He gained French citizenship in 1938, but because of his Jewish heritage, he and his family were soon forced to flee France to the United States. Settled in Los Angeles, Tansman became acquainted with Schoenberg and composed a number of film scores. He returned to Paris in 1946. His honors included the Coolidge Medal (1941), election to the Académie Royale of Belgium (1977) and the Polish Medal of Cultural Merit (1983). He composed hundreds of pieces in total, exploring practically every musical genre, from symphonies to ballets to chamber music and works for solo guitar.

POINTS FOR PRACTICE AND TEACHING

Ping Pong / *Ping-Pong*
from For Children, Volume 3 / *Pour les enfants, volume 3*
Alexandre Tansman

- Note the nearly constant staccato articulations. These are essential for capturing the ping pong inspiration for the piece.
- Tansman cleverly creates a back-and-forth dialogue between the right and L.H. similar to two players hitting a ping pong ball. The volley between players first alternates every two beats, and then in m. 3-4 it speeds up to every beat.
- A common motive in the piece is an alteration between fifths and thirds. Both hands get a chance to work on changing between these intervals.
- Practice the hands together and work on an absolute evenness of tempo.
- There are several dramatic changes of dynamics. Note the sudden *f* at m. 13 and p at m. 25.
- The R.H. is completely exposed in m. 13-16. Remember to keep *staccato* articulation on every note.
- Though piece is written mostly in D minor, it ends unexpectedly in D Major. Who won the game?

Prayer / *Prière*
from Ten Diversions for the Young Pianist / *Dix Récréations pour le jeune pianist*
Alexandre Tansman

- In this piece Tansman seems to imitate French organ composers of the Romantic era, like Franck or Widor. The long sustained chords and delicate dissonances contribute to a very solemn, indeed organ-like, mood.
- When playing organ, there is no sustain pedal to catch notes; you have to continue holding each key that will sound. Though you can make use of the piano's pedal here, try to keep the spirit of this music by connecting notes through legato playing.
- Some of the L.H.'s stretches may prove difficult. See the sevenths with inner voices in m. 7-8, 9-11, 14-16, and 30.
- M. 13 requires the L.H. to reach as far as a ninth, but notice how the inner voices pass from L.H. to R.H.
- Note the sequence of descending fifths in the L.H. m. 17-19. If it is too hard to use the fourth finger on these chords, a 5-1 fingering for all chords is acceptable.
- Lift after the downbeat of m. 21 to move to the new hand position.

Greetings / *Présentations*
from Ten Easy Little Pieces / *Dix Petites Pièces Faciles*
Charles Koechlin

- Koechlin wrote this piece without a time signature, but we have added a time signature of 4/4 and dotted barlines as guides.
- Pay attention to the frequent changes between eighth notes and triplets.
- In m. 6-7, both hands are notated in the treble staff. Practice the hands separately here to confirm which notes are in each voice.
- After mostly light textures throughout, m. 10-11 are suddenly more complicated. Practice hands separately and as slowly as necessary. In performance, use the "Very slow" tempo marking at m. 10 to your advantage.
- The quintuplet in the last measure is essentially a written-out ornament.
- The piece has a spirit of pleasantry and goodwill between two friends.

Franz / *Franz*
Olivier Hauray

- The "Franz" of the title probably refers to Franz Schubert, a late Classical/early Romantic composer. The style resembles one of Schubert's lively dance miniatures.
- The L.H. has some large leaps to low bass notes. These demand a strong, focused fifth finger. Practice the L.H. line slowly, and also try to reach a point where you can accurately make the long leaps without looking. In time you will gain a sense of where the low notes are.
- Carefully practice the R.H.'s tricky fingering in m. 10-12.

Gymnopédie No. 1 / *Gymnopédie No. 1*
from Three Gymnopédies / *Trois Gymnopédies*
Erik Satie

- The word Gymnopédie might refer to a type of ancient Greek ritual dance performed by young men.
- This is Satie's most famous piece. You might even recognize it from an appearance in a film or TV commercial.
- Maintain a calm steadiness to create the piece's serene spirit.
- Notice that almost every bar has a pattern of a low note on the downbeat followed by a chord on beat 2.
- Some accompaniment notes have been marked with brackets to show that they can be played by the R.H.
- Keep a smooth legato in the R.H. melody.
- Pedal on each downbeat.

Tyrolean Waltz / *Valse tyrolienne*
from The Villagers / *Villageoises*
Francis Poulenc

- The word "Tyrolean" means pertaining to the state of Tyrol, in the Alps of western Austria.
- The R.H. has a wide-ranging melody while the L.H. provides oom-pah-pah waltz accompaniment.
- Practice jumping to the L.H.'s low bass notes slowly and, eventually, without looking.
- Notice that the L.H. begins holds the bass notes in m. 17-30 through each full measure.
- Keep a graceful melody in the R.H.
- Keep a steady L.H. accompaniment, always softer than the R.H., and try to relax to keep the music from sounding too busy or frantic.
- In m. 31-32 Poulenc has written a deliberately dissonant crunch in the music. Have fun with this moment!

Staccato / *Staccato*
from The Villagers / *Villageoises*
Francis Poulenc

- This piece certainly earns its title with nearly constant *staccato* chords and bass accompaniment. Note the opening expression "very dry," emphasizing the *staccato* sound.
- The R.H. melody descending by half step, combined with the tuba-like bass line, combine to create the atmosphere of a circus or carnival. Poulenc had a penchant for these whimsical musical moods.
- Notice the accents on the first beats of m. 2, 4, etc. In a piece where almost every note is *staccato*, these special accents should stand out.
- In m. 17-24, the texture suddenly thins to a single line. Make sure to observe all the articulations in the R.H. line. This includes the breath marks (apostrophes) in m. 20 and m. 22. Poulenc wants a slight rest in the music at those points.
- There are many dramatic changes of dynamics. Notice the sudden *f* at m. 176 after an opening section marked p. The single most dramatic change is in m. 22-24, where you must *crescendo* from *p* to *f* and back to *p* in a very short amount of time.
- The thirty-second notes in m. 20-21 should define the tempo you choose for the piece. Make sure you can play these quickly and crisply at your tempo.

Paul and Virginia / *Paul et Virginie*
from Poetic Pieces, Book 2 / *Pièces Poetiques (deuxième cahier)*
Henri Sauguet

- This piece has a lovely melancholy mood that makes you wonder about the relationship of the two characters of the title.
- Apply a soft tone to the three repeated notes of the melody, without poking.
- From m. 9 into m. 10, the R.H. has a new type of finger cross: the third finger crosses over the fifth. Practice this slowly.
- Even at a slow tempo, the more active L.H. accompaniment in m. 10-15 demands agility and a sure sense of your next hand position. Note the *sim.* indication after m. 10; the fingerings in that measure can be used for m. 11-12 as well.
- The L.H. has another tricky passage in m. 14-15. To master the basic movement, try playing just the fourth finger on B below middle C, then jumping up to the next B. Jump back and forth slowly until you can accurately make the leap at tempo.
- The *ritenuto* in m. 15-16 is a gradual slowing down of the music. Practice this until it is not musically awkward.

- When the main melody returns in m. 17, notice how the R.H. line is now harmonized into two-note chords. Despite the thicker texture, keep the dynamic **pp** as marked.
- In the last measure, notice that only the F-sharps in both hands are held to the end.

Mystery / *Mystère*
Oliver Hauray

- Notice the time signature of 3/4 + 4/4. The true time signature is 7/4, but Hauray is showing how it divides. At the most basic level, the feel is 3+2+2. We have added dotted barlines to assist in following the meter.
- Every measure of the piece begins with the same motive. Because of this, make sure to explicitly follow all dynamics to keep the music interesting and varied.
- To create an arc to the music, think of each two-bar group as a question followed by an answer.
- There is a rather consistent pattern of a *f* statement of the main motive followed by a held chord marked *p*.
- In m. 9-10, the main motive is imitated between hands in a canonlike way, one beat apart.
- In m. 12-14, the L.H. chords are played very close to the R.H.'s ending notes. Experiment with crossing the L.H. over or under the right and find a comfortable solution.
- Notice that in m. 14, the R.H. is still *forte*, continuing the pattern of *f* followed by *p* held notes.

Lullaby / *Berceuse*
from Ten Easy Little Pieces / *Dix Petites Pièces Faciles*
Charles Koechlin

- Koechlin wrote this piece with no barlines or time signature. We have added both as guides.
- The key signature of B Major may be foreign to some players at this level. Practice or study B Major scales to ease into the key.
- Practice the R.H. alone without pedal, to ensure that the two-voice sections are as clear and *legato* as possible.
- Notice the different phrase lengths. Most of these are quite long. Do your best to carry the melody line all the way through.
- The L.H. has a gentle rocking accompaniment, but the thumb often has to reach very high for top notes. Try to relax and reach for these with a smooth motion. Avoid overly accenting the top notes.

Skipping / *Trottinez "Martin"*
from For Small Hands / *Petites mains*
Pierre Sancan

- In the twentieth century and onward, composers felt free to experiment with unconventional harmonies and melodies. Try to embrace the new sounds you'll encounter here.
- Sancan uses a variety of articulations in this piece. The recurring L.H. accompaniment of *staccato* notes often has an accent on the first note of each bar, and the grace note figures land on notes marked *tenuto*.
- The dynamics range from *f* to **pp**, with many *crescendos* and *decrescendos*. Observe these dynamics for added color.
- In m. 12-21, the R.H. has repeated eighth notes with a changing finger pattern. Practice this slowly and work your way up to the tempo. The alternating fingering is the best solution for this situation; playing the same finger repeatedly at this tempo may lead to unwanted tension.
- In sections with repeated chords instead of single notes, as in m. 1-12 in the L.H., practice slowly with a loose wrist to achieve a pecking motion low to the keys.
- Notice the melodic fragments that appear in the R.H. in m. 24-27, then are restated in the L.H. in m. 29-32. Sancan instructs us to bring out the left melody so the imitative effect is clear to the listener.
- Between the complicated-sounding dissonances and the fast-paced action, this piece will sound impressive in performance!

Sound the Drum / *Résonnez "Tambour"*
from For Small Hands / *Petites mains*
Pierre Sancan

- If you played "Skipping," you'll be familiar with Sancan's spiky musical language. This piece also includes some of the same repeated staccato notes and chords.
- Sancan creates a strict military feel with a bass pattern repeated through m. 1-5 and triplet grace notes that recall snare drum rolls. Keep the rhythms absolutely precise and in tempo.
- No pedal should be used in this exceptionally dry (or *secco*) piece.
- Sancan has marked small *decrescendos* on the first two triplet grace notes. Accent the first note and then quickly back off.
- Be careful to observe differing articulations at spots like m. 20-27, with *staccato* in one hand and *tenuto* in the other.
- The section in m. 28-37 serves as a review of techniques in other pieces in this book: repeated notes in the R.H. with alternating fingering, repeated chords in the L.H. with frequent fingering changes, and a variety of articulations to execute.
- The fingerings given for the L.H. chords in m. 30-37 can be modified for different preferences. The fingering change from beat 1 to beat 2 of m. 30 is meant to relieve the tension of repetitive motion.
- Notice the marking *poco a poco dim.* starting at m. 42. Lower the volume bit by bit until the music fades away at the end.

Candy / *Les bonbons*
from A Child Loves / *L'Enfant Aime*
Darius Milhaud

- Milhaud's music takes many unexpected turns. This piece is sweet like candy, but also unpredictable. At the very least, m. 1-4 and m. 36-39 have the exact same material.
- It is essential to follow the written phrasing to shape the unusual turns of melody.
- Don't worry about a soft tone when first learning this piece. Play confidently at first, and then adjust the volume later when you have mastered the notes.
- Notice the many specific pedal instructions. In the 1/4 markings, Milhaud is calling for the pedal to be depressed partially, not fully. This is a rather sophisticated technique that occurs rarely in music of this level.
- M. 7 features another pedal instruction: *una corda*. Instead of pressing down the sustain pedal, press the left-most pedal. This achieves a thin, delicate sound. The phrase *una corda* means "one string"; this pedal shifts the position of the hammers in the piano so that they only strike one piano string per note instead of three.
- Pay attention to the measures that begin with rests: m. 5, 7, 19, 21, 40, and 42. Try counting "1" to yourself silently in time and feel the entrance on beat 2.

Games in the Park / *Ronde dans le Parc*
from On Vacation, Volume 1 / *En vacances, 1er recueil*
Deodat de Séverac

- Despite the title, the character is more noble than fun, with a stately melody.
- Notice how m. 9-17 are a varied version of m. 1-8.
- The two hands play many similar rhythms, and the lack of a developed accompaniment gives this the feel of a chorale or hymn.
- Séverac has written many specific pedal indications. Wherever you see alternating and [*] signs, reset the pedal on each chord to keep each new harmony clean. From beat 2 of m. 21 to beat 1 of m. 24, use no pedal.
- Notice the R.H. chords in m. 2-3 and m. 42-43 with both *staccato* and *tenuto* marks. These chords can be played as slightly extended *staccatos*, with about half of the chord's full value.
- Practice the L.H. cross of the third finger over the fifth finger in m. 26-27.

Dreams / *Rêves*

from Ten Diversions for the Young Pianist / *Dix Récréations pour le jeune pianist*

Alexandre Tansman

- If you played Tansman's piece "Little Dream" from the Early Intermediate level of this series, you may notice a similarity in the musical texture.
- To better manage this sea of notes, it may help to know that m. 1-6 and m. 17-22 contain the same music.
- Some pedal is necessary to sustain tones while giving yourself time to jump to new hand positions.
- Both hands must learn to move gracefully between positions, retaining the calm mood Tansman has asked for.
- Notice the slurs on every two-note phrase in the L.H., as well as most of the R.H. You can lift off the previous note for an easier reach. The pedal will also aid this movement.
- Keep the R.H. slightly more prominent than the left, treating it as a melody. Do not overly accent L.H. phrases.
- Be ready for the rhythmic pattern change at m. 10.
- Even though you are playing single notes in each hand, notice that these are outlining chords.

Siciliana / *Sicilienne*

from Ten Easy Little Pieces / *Dix Petites Pièces Faciles*

Charles Koechlin

- A *siciliana* (or *sicilienne*) is a slow dance from the Baroque era in 6/8 time, characterized by dotted rhythms.
- While this piece was originally notated without a time signature or barlines, we have added both to aid in counting and to emphasize the 6/8 feel.
- Notice the lengths of phrases, particularly the four-measure phrases in m. 5-8, 11-14, and 15-18. Try to carry the melody through each phrase.
- Watch for places where the two hands swap rhythms. In m. 3, 9, 16, and 21, the R.H. has a dotted rhythm on beat 1 while the L.H. has straight eighth notes, but on beat 2 the R.H. plays eighths and the L.H. has the dotted rhythm.
- Koechlin calls for some bottom L.H. notes to sustain through entire measures, requiring creative fingering and independence of fingers. Do your best with the finger crosses in m. 1-2, 9-10, 11-13, and 15-21.
- Some of the notes in the bass staff in m. 13 can be taken by the R.H. if necessary.
- In m. 11, the somber music turns lighter and more hopeful in the parallel key of A Major. Notice the tempo is "a bit more animated." This should be just a slight increase in speed.
- After a return to the original minor-key mood in m. 19, the piece ends on an A Major sonority. Koechlin, though writing in the twentieth century, has imitated a popular stylistic choice in Baroque music.

Prélude / *Prélude*

Maurice Ravel

- French style in the Impressionist period requires sophistication of touch, phrasing, pedaling and musicality.
- This piece is about elegant, languorous phrase and lush harmony.
- Play the eighth note figures throughout very smoothly.
- Pay careful attention to Ravel's phrase markings.
- In m. 10–15, the hands are close together, with the R.H. playing on top of the L.H.
- The rolled chord in the R.H. in measure 16 and 18 will take some practice for most hands. If your hand is too small to hold all the notes down after they are rolled, then experiment with letting one or two of the notes go, sustaining the sound with careful use of the sustaining pedal.
- Pedal needs to be applied. Be careful to keep the harmonies clear. Do make this or any other Impressionist piece a vague blur of sound.

Spanish Mood / *Atmosphère espagnole*
from Ten Diversions for the Young Pianist / *Dix Récréations pour le jeune pianist*
Alexandre Tansman

- Tansman captures a little bit of Spanish flavor here, but the piece still has a French sound overall.
- Even though there are no phrase markings in the L.H. for the first eight bars, the line should still be played *legato*, as marked.
- Use plenty of pedal in this piece, changing enough to prevent harmonies from blurring.
- M. 22 features a very surprising harmonic turn. Make it seem spontaneous.
- In m. 10-11 and m. 14-16, the top A's and G's in the L.H. should both be played by the thumb. Practice a smooth, gentle alternation between these notes, without poking.

The Little Cartoon Cat / *Le Petit Chat des dessins animés*
from For Children, Volume 2 / *Pour les enfants, volume 2*
Alexandre Tansman

- It is uncertain which cartoon cat Tansman refers to in the title, but try to imagine your own.
- The two hands have an interlocking pattern that requires management of space; keep the hands arched enough to prevent collisions. Practice the hands together slowly.
- Keep the constant sixteenth notes steady and rhythmic.
- This piece sounds harder than it is to play, and can be quite fun and satisfying when played up to tempo.
- The L.H.'s leap up into the treble register and the cross over the right in m. 8 will look very impressive in performance.
- M. 14-15 contain a long descending sequence. Practice each hand separately. The fingering on the first figures in both hands can be used for the rest of the sequence.

Difficult Problem / *Problème difficile*
from For Children, Volume 3 / *Pour les enfants, volume 3*
Alexandre Tansman

- This is one of several Tansman pieces that imitates Baroque style, with independent parts between the hands and use of musical sequences.
- The intricate fingering and contrapuntal nature of this piece present difficult problems indeed. Practice hands slowly and separately.
- Use no pedal at all. Make sure the fingers can produce *legato* articulation on their own.
- Notice how m. 13-16 are a repeat of m. 1-4, but an octave higher.
- Work up to a performance tempo that feels comfortable and keep it steady, without rushing.

– Brendan Fox
editor

Bonjour,
Piano!

Ping Pong

from *For Children*, Volume 3

Alexandre Tansman

3

Prayer
from *Ten Diversions for the Young Pianist*

Alexandre Tansman

Andante espressivo [♩ = c. 76–80]

Greetings
from *Ten Easy Little Pieces*

Charles Koechlin

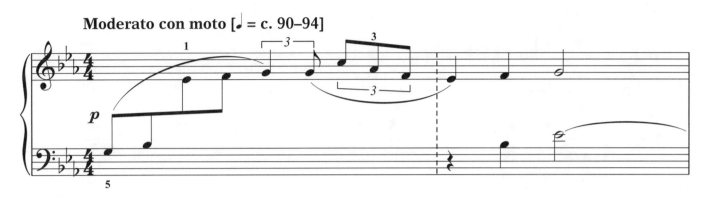

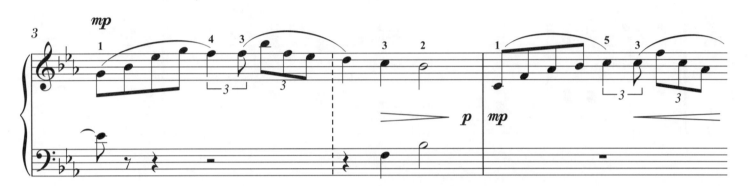

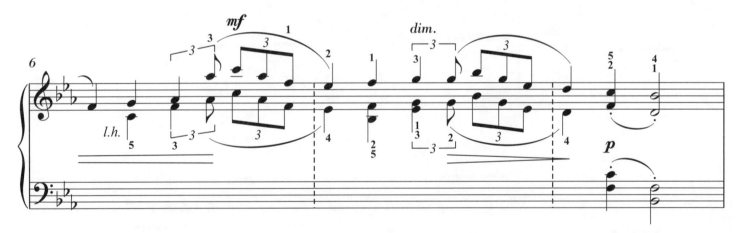

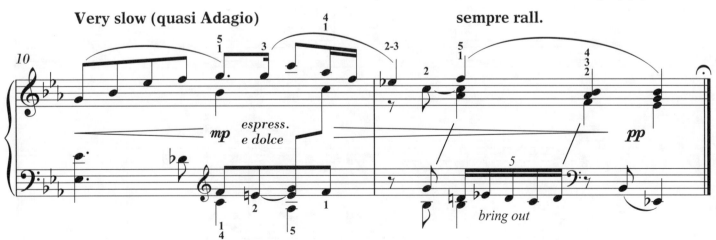

The time signature and the dotted barlines are editorial suggestions.

© Éditions SALABERT
Paris, France

Franz

Olivier Hauray

Semplice [♩ = c. 104–110]

à Mademoiselle Jeanne de Bret

Gymnopédie No. 1

from *Three Gymnopédies*

Erik Satie

Tyrolean Waltz

from *The Villagers*

Francis Poulenc

without slowing down

Staccato

from *The Villagers*

Francis Poulenc

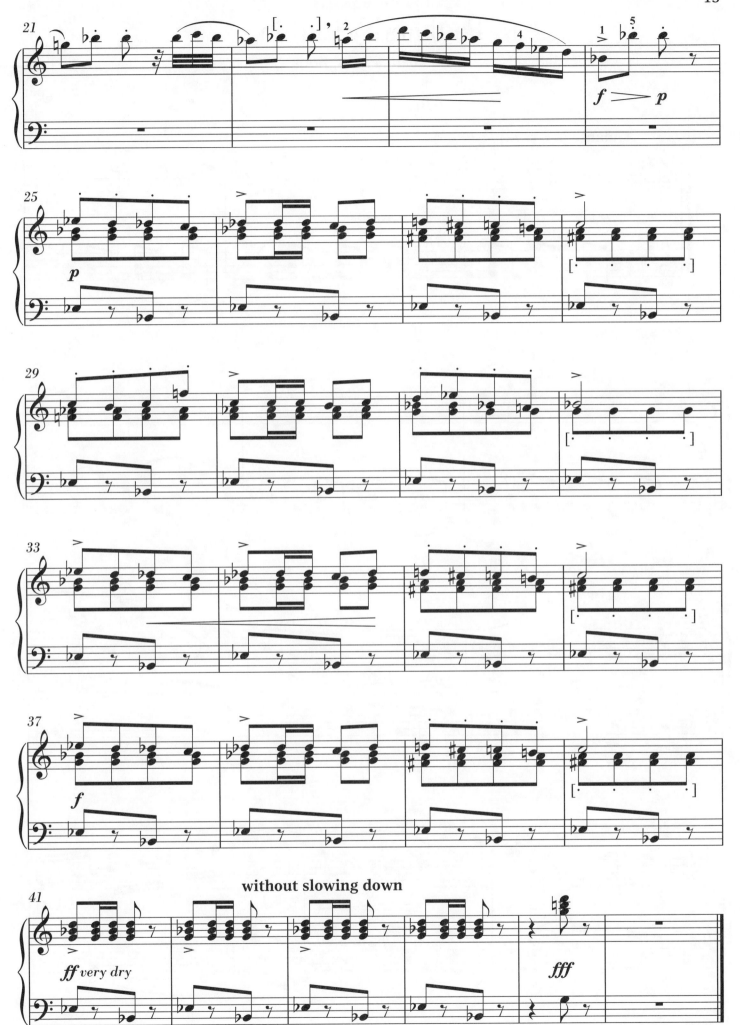

without slowing down

à Natalie de Noailles

Paul and Virginia

from *Poetic Pieces*, Book 2

Henri Sauguet

ri -

- te - nu - to

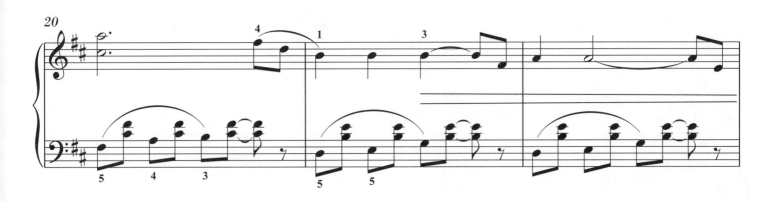

Mystery

Olivier Hauray

Lullaby
from *Ten Easy Little Pieces*

Charles Koechlin

The time signature and barlines are editorial suggestions.

Skipping

from *For Small Hands*

Pierre Sancan

Sound the Drum

from *For Small Hands*

Pierre Sancan

Candy

from *A Child Loves*

Darius Milhaud

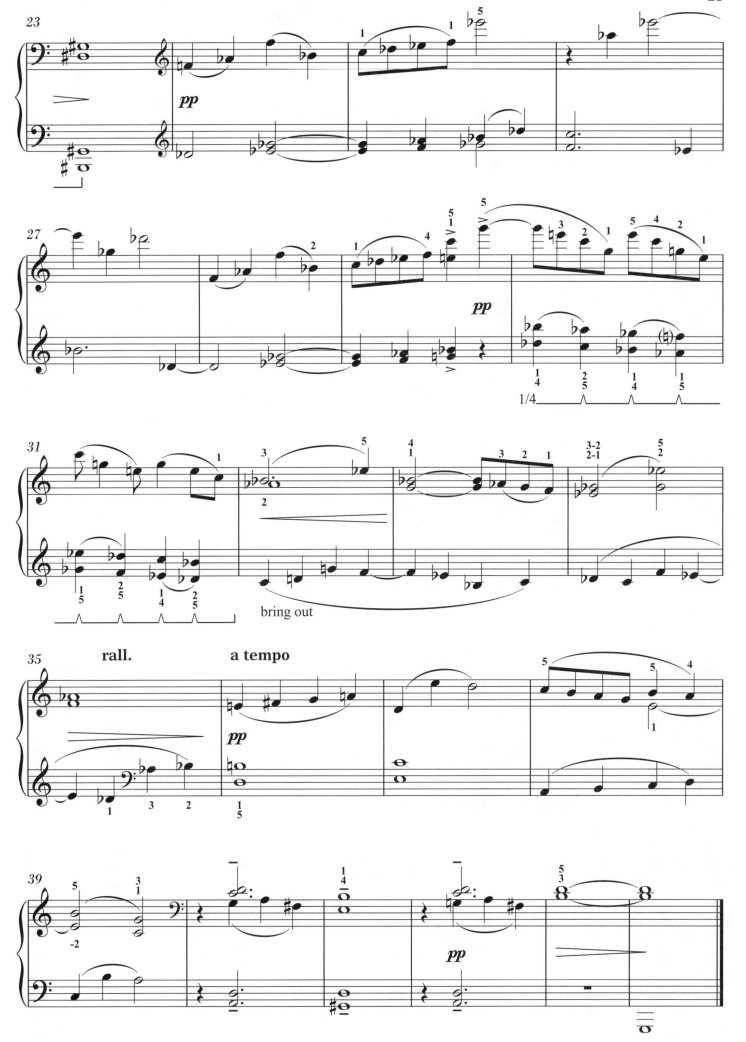

Games in the Park

from *On Vacation*, Volume 1

Déodat de Séverac

Dreams

from *Ten Diversions for the Young Pianist*

Alexandre Tansman

Andante grazioso [♩ = c. 76–80]

Siciliana
from *Ten Easy Little Pieces*

Charles Koechlin

The time signature and barlines are editorial suggestions.

à Mademoiselle Jeanne Leleu

Prélude

Maurice Ravel

Quite slow and very expressive (with free rhythm) [♩ = c. 60]

with pedal

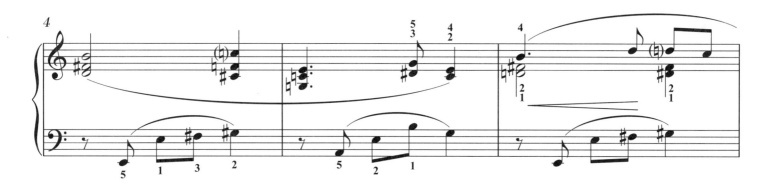

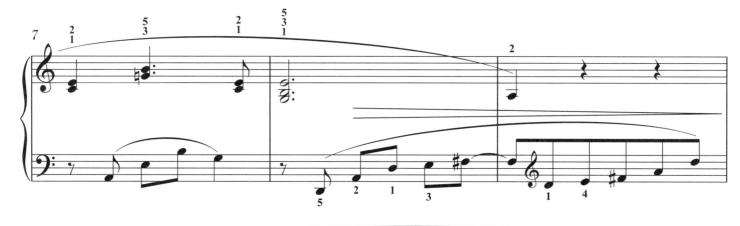

Fingerings are editorial additions.

Spanish Mood

from *Ten Diversions for the Young Pianist*

Alexandre Tansman

Andante, espressivo [♩ = c. 76]

The Little Cartoon Cat

from *For Children*, Volume 2

Alexandre Tansman

Moderately (or fairly lively) [♩ = c. 76–80]

Difficult Problem

from *For Children*, Volume 3

Alexandre Tansman

Fairly lively [♩ = c. 88–92]